Unique Creatures
Of The World

By: Angelica Marie Morales

Lions

The first animal we will be talking about is a Lion. Lions have sharp teeth. Some Lions have teeth up to Three inches long! These big teeth are used for ripping through thick meat such as Zebra skin, Deer, Ox, Fish, and sometimes humans. If another type of animal try's to harm it the Lion might snap back and show its big teeth so the other animal or human gets frightened and runs away. Lions are most known for their fur. Male Lions have thick fur that gets nappy and tight. Female Lions have straight short hair that

Doesn't get nappy or tight. Lions also have long tails. Their tails are about 36 inches long (1 yard), sometimes shorter. It depends on how old the Lion is and how its eating. Lions come from Africa and Asia where they originated. They live an average of 15 years.

Tigers

Tigers are related to Lions. They're both in the cat family. If you have a cat you might be thinking, "My cats related to a Tiger?" Well the answer is yes! All cats are related to Lions and Tigers. Tigers are orange, black, and white just like a clown fish. Tigers mostly live in Southern Asia near the Rainforest. Their teeth are three to two inches long. Tigers eat meat, leaves, grass, and sometimes humans if you bother them. I have to say they're really nice if you don't bother them. Their hairs don't grow as much like male lions. They have hair like female lions, which helps them feel cool in the hot, hot, sun. Tigers are most known for their beauty. They are beautiful animals witch makes people admire them in zoos. Many tigers have green, blue, amber, and hazel eye color just like some house cats.

Red Eye Tree Frogs

Red Eye Tree Frogs have red eyes witch give them the first part of their names. They also love playing on trees that's what gives them their second part of their names. They live in Costa Rica, Southern Mexico and Northern Colombia, in the rainforest.

You might not want to touch them because their urine might give you warts … Yuck! I know I wouldn't like being touched by one of them! They're about two to three Inches long! That's about the size of one domino! Red eye tree frogs are green with a pad of yellow on their stomachs. Many people have them as pets but if you take them out of their habitat they wont live very long. They must live in 75 to 85 degrees during the day and 65 to 75 degree weather at night. Females are 51 to 71 mm long and males are 30 to 59 mm. They live an average of 30.

Pandas

Pandas are famous for their habitat and their color. Pandas are from China. That's right near Japan. An earthquake appeared in Japan, but I'm sure glad none of these pandas got hurt! Pandas are one of the most famous animals in the world! They're famous because many people like seeing them walk around, with their stomachs wobbling everywhere. They are also furry witch makes people want to jump right on them and snuggle! Pandas eat bamboo. Bamboo is a type of plant that is crunchy. Pandas like bamboo because of its crunchy feeling just like celery sticks! I think they'd love those as much as I do!

Giraffes

Giraffes are tall animals! They can be up to sixteen to Eighteen feet tall and weigh up to 1,361 kilograms, 3,000 in pounds. That's taller than a tree and heavier than a Gorilla! There so tall I bet they can touch the sky! Giraffes don't sleep much. They mostly sleep up to 10 minutes in a 24-hour period. They have lots of bones. I'm not even sure how many bones it has! Giraffes have stubby tails. Their very small but they have lots of small bones in it. The Skull is really different then other animals. The skull is shaped in a triangle form. The top of it is in a rectangle form. And the eye sockets are ovals.

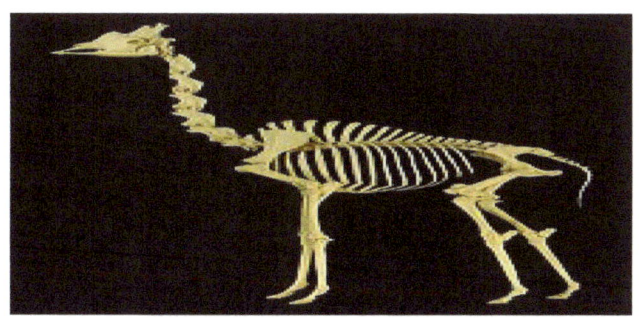

Toucans

Toucans are beautiful birds, and one of my favorites! Some toucans have rainbow beaks, and some of them just have mango colored beaks. Toucans live in Puerto Rico and in Other hot Islands. Toucans love to eat berries, mangos, bananas, grapefruit, watermelon, lemons, limes, strawberries, blueberries, pineapple, pears, apples, and oranges. Toucans are not very strong. They have small wings. Instead of using their wings for flying, they use them for griping onto branches.

Sharks

Sharks are sneaky and smart animals. When they feel something or someone coming they get

Ready and make an army of sharks and fight. Sharks are cold blooded. They are fierce and fast to catch there pray. They eat lots of meat. They eat fish, rays, other small sharks, and human. They are NOT safe to go around. If you ever see a sign near an ocean, read it before going in the water! Sharks are over 5,000 pounds! And can grow about 25 feet long. The Whale shark has 3 rows of teeth and in each row are 300 teeth! Most Whale sharks don't eat human, but they do eat other type of fish.

Camels

Camels are most known for their impressive water storing humps that are prominent in the camel's back. Camels are mainly found in the Middle – East, and in some areas of eastern Asia. Camels are incredibly resilient to the desert climates and the arid conditions that would easily kill another animal. Camels also posses the incredible ability to lose nearly 40% of their body weight as water and be unharmed.

Snakes

There are over 2,700 known species of snake worldwide. The snake can grow up to 10cm in length, to the enormous anaconda snake that can reach lengths of up to 30ft long! There are two ways that snakes kill there pray, either the snake has poisonous bite or the snake will wrap its self around the pray to constrict it.

Eagles

Eagles are famous because they represent the United States of America. Eagles live in warm forests and they eat raspberries, blue berry, seeds, cherries, cherry pits, peaches, and lots more fruit and berries. Eagles have long beautiful wings. They can fly up to 50ft high in the air! They glide more than flying. Their feet have long pointy nails that grip onto thick and thin branches.

Siamese Fighting Fish

The Siamese fighting Fish is very colorful. It always changes color! If it's red, it will turn orange. If it's blue, it will change green, but when the Siamese fighting fish gets mad their whole bodies turn red and its cheeks puff up. They don't need air as much as they need water. They can spend about 5 minutes under water without floating up for air. I have to say these fish sure are healthy and very different then other fish.

Kangaroos

Kangaroos are very mixed animals. They have ears like wolfs, tails like a Tyrannosaurus Rex, legs like a horse, noses like dogs, necks like a deer, and feet like Eagles. But one thing that is different about them then other animals are there deep pouches. When their babies are born, the baby rests in the pouch and grows. The kangaroo stays in the pouch until its old enough to wonder outside alone.

Baby Kangaroo

Polar Bears

Polar bears are white fuzzy bears with black eyes and black noses! Polar bears are from the Arctic. They slide and glide on icy icebergs and swim in the big Pacific Ocean. Polar bears are related a brown bear. Just like brown bears, they love to eat fish. Polar bears have short white Fur witch is very warm for them. But you might be thinking, "there's no way they can stay warm with really short fur." Well that's wrong! Polar bears have fat under their fur witch makes them real hot.

Rhinoceros

Rhinoceros are very awkward animals. They have horns like Triceratops, and a body like a Hippopotamus. Some people think this animal is a dinosaur. Is it true? Is the animal so called a Rhinoceros an animal or a dinosaur? Many people are still trying to find out this mystery.

Alligators

Alligators are much smaller than Crocodiles. Crocodiles are much, much bigger than Alligators. Alligators are very vicious animals. They like to bite lots of things, and love crawling around in lakes and swamps. They live in forests, ponds, lakes, and swamps. Their teeth are about 1 to 2 inches long. They are 4 to 6 feet long. Alligators are awesome at doing lots of things. Some Alligators are trained to do tricks and to not bite people.

Lynx

Lynx's are the one wildest cat in the Cat family. Lynx's are most known for their stubby tails and long black hair on the tip of their ears. There are different types of Lynx with these being in North America, Canada, and Alaska. The European Lynx found in Spain and Portugal. Lynx's are carnivores witch means they mostly eat meat, and their favorite food is Hare witch another name for a rabbit.

Cheetahs

Cheetahs are very popular around the USA. When lots of people think of wild animals they mostly think of cheetahs. Cheetahs are most known for the pattern on their body and their speed. They have light brown colors with black dots all around them. Most cheetahs have brown eyes. That's because of its body color. Most animals have eye color that match their body color, and cheetahs seem to have that. Cheetahs have very sharp teeth. Sometimes their bodies grow so big, that their teeth grow twice as much! That's about 4 to 5 inches long! What a big mouth! All Cheetahs run 70 miles per Hour! That's fast!

Hyenas

Hahahaha! Hyenas love to laugh! They laugh for a special reason. Sometimes they laugh to warn other hyenas, and if they need to huddle up. Hyenas are about the size of a large dog. That's about 20 to 30 inches long or if the hyena would stand up on its hind legs, it would be about 4 feet high. That's about the size of a 9 or 10 year old child. They have medium size tails, and very small ears. Some people think they have pointy ears but there probably thinking of a Lynx.

Flamingos

Flamingos are beautiful long legged birds. They come in all different colors even blue! Flamingos have long legs and long necks. With their long neck and long legs they are able to drink water without having to bend down. They have colorful wings but they can't fly! Their wings are mostly used for cooling them selves down.

Bottle Nosed Dolphins

Bottle nosed Dolphins are most common and well known type of Dolphin. Bottle nosed Dolphins are found inhabiting warm seas worldwide. Many people love bottle nosed Dolphins because of their talent. They are trained for helping people and making them feel happy! Like other Whales and Dolphins, Bottle nosed Dolphins eat fish and plankton. Plankton is a small, small, small creature that floats above the water. They're so small that you'll need a magnified glass to see them!

Elephants

Elephants are Huge! Elephants are herbivores that spend about 22 hours eating! They mostly eat long green leaves. Elephants have tusks. Tusks are the long bones on their faces. It's also known as ivory tusk. People cut off their tusks to make different things.

Elephants have long eyelashes that wave up and down to flick flies off their eyes. That's one thing Camels and elephants have in common.

Sea Dragon

The sea dragon is a small, delicate fish found in the tropical coastal waters of south and west Australia. Sea Dragons look similar to and are in fact closely related to Sea Horses, that's awesome!

Leafy sea Dragon

There are two different species of sea dragon, which are the leafy sea dragon and the weedy sea dragon. Although both sea dragon species have a similar body shape and size, they are very different in appearance.

Armadillo

The armadillo has very poor vision that makes the armadillo somewhat vulnerable in its jungle environment. Plates of bone covered in relatively small overlapping scales form the armadillo's armor. The scales of the armadillo are known as scutes and these scutes are made up of bone with a covering of horn.

The armadillo has additional armor that covers the top of its head, the upper parts of the armadillo's limbs and the armadillo's tail. The underside of the armadillo has no armor, and is simply covered with soft skin and fur, hence it's strategy of curling into a ball leaving only the armored plates exposed.

Zebra

Zebra's are sadly an endangered species and there are only a few left in the wild. The zebra is best known for the black and white striping pattern unique to each of the 3 species of zebra. Within a species, the pattern of the stripes is unique to each individual zebra, like with a human's fingerprint. There is some evidence that zebras recognize herd mates by their patterns. The female zebra usually gives birth to just one zebra foal after a 12 month gestation period. Female zebras have been known to give birth to zebra twins but it is a fairly fair occurrence. Zebra foals are able to stand and run about just hours after birth and remain close the mother zebra until they are big enough to look out for themselves.

Bobcat

Bobcats are widespread and adaptable predators across North America. They share the genus Lynx with the Canadian Lynx, but they are a separate species with physical differences. Bobcats are usually more heavily spotted than the lynx. They have smaller feet and larger ears. They tend to have a more aggressive temperament and have been known to run the much larger Lynx off of food. The bobcat's ears do have small tufts on the end like those of the lynx. Although the bobcat shares many characteristics with the Canadian Lynx the bobcat is smaller than the lynx at about double the size of a domestic cat.

Snowy Owl

The snowy owl is also known as the Arctic owl or the great white owl. The snowy owl is primarily found within the Arctic Circle with the range of the snowy owl ranging across Canada, Greenland, Europe and Asia. The snowy owl is the official bird of Quebec in the Northeast of Canada.

The snowy owl is one of the largest species of owl in the world, with the average adult snowy owl growing to about 65cm tall with a wingspan of around 140cm. Snowy owls however can be smaller than this, and can even grow to more than 75cm in height.

Sponge

Sponges are very slow moving animals that are found across the sea floor. Although many sponges actually move less than a millimeter a day, some adult sponges are actually sessile, which means that they are fixed onto something and do not move at all. Sponges are thought to have evolved around 500 million years ago, and today there are more than 5,000 known species of sponge with another 5,000 species thought to have not yet been discovered. Most sponges live in a salt-water environment, attached to objects on the sea floor. Less than 200 sponge species inhabit fresh water habitats.

Catfish

Catfish are a group of bottom-feeding fish that are found in fresh water and coastal regions on and around every continent in the world with the exception of Antarctica. Their flattened broad heads and the long whisker-like barbells that protrude from the mouth of the catfish most easily identify catfish.

The long barbells of the catfish contain the taste buds of the catfish and so are often most commonly used for smelling and therefore sensing what is about to eat and to hide from in the surrounding waters. Despite the name however, not all catfish species have prominent whisker-like barbells.

Pond Skater

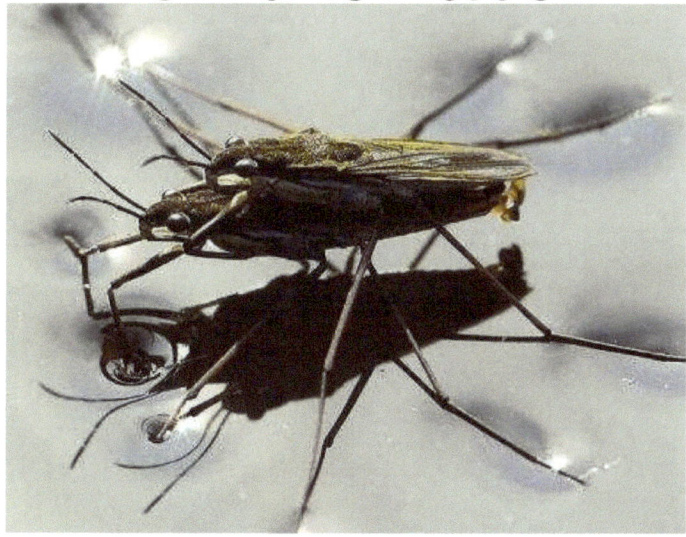

The pond skater is a delicate water-based insect commonly found on still bodies of water across the Northern Hemisphere. There are around 500 different species of pond skater that are known by a variety of different names including water strides, water bugs, magic bugs, skaters, skimmers, water scooters, water skaters, water skitters, water skimmers, water skippers and Jesus bugs.

The pond skater is most commonly found across Europe where they live on the surface of ponds, slow streams, marshes, and other quiet waters, in all parts of the continent. Pond skaters are most well known for their ability to "walk on water", where pond skaters use surface tension to delicately walk on the surface of the water.

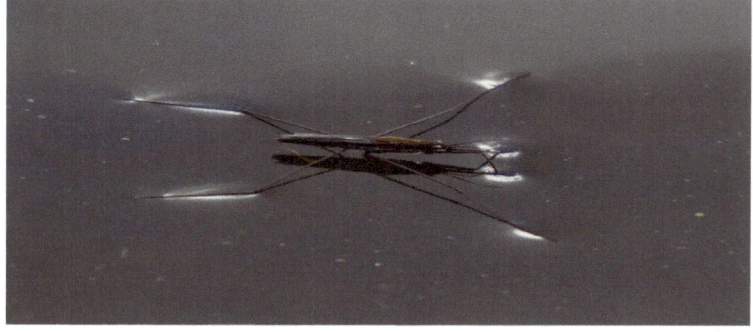

Aye Aye

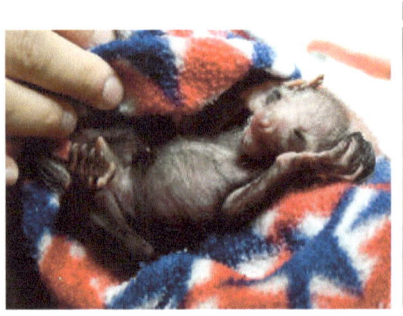  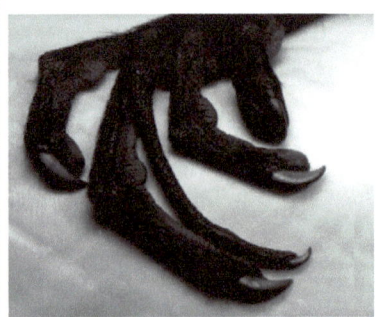

The aye aye monkey is a subspecies of lemur found on the southeastern African Island of Madagascar. The aye aye monkey is the biggest nocturnal primate in the world with some aye aye monkey weighing more than 3kg! The aye aye monkey is also one of the few solitary species of primate and therefore hunts alone for grubs and insects. The aye aye has rodent-like teeth and a long, thin middle finger that fills the same ecological niche as a woodpecker The aye aye taps on trees to find grubs then gnaws holes in the wood and inserts its long middle finger into the hole to pull the grubs out. The aye aye is considered to be a near threatened species, possibly even endangered with very few aye ayes left in the wild. The second subspecies of aye aye monkey is thought to have become extinct at some point in the past 1,000 years.

INDEX